Original title:
Forest Bathing

Copyright © 2024 Swan Charm
All rights reserved.

Editor: Jessica Elisabeth Luik
Author: Paulina Pähkel
ISBN HARDBACK: 978-9916-86-437-1
ISBN PAPERBACK: 978-9916-86-438-8

Roots and Whisperings

In soil deep, where stories weave,
Silent songs the earth does grieve.
Ancient roots in darkness twine,
Secrets kept by old wood's spine.

Whispered tales of time's embrace,
Echoes laced with nature's grace.
Binding life, unseen yet known,
In their grasp, the seeds are sown.

Through the quiet, whispers spread,
Language of the leaves is read.
Nature's prose in breezes light,
Roots and branches hold the night.

Leafy Embrace

Arms of green reach through the sky,
Touching clouds where dreams do fly.
In the shade, a cool caress,
Nature's touch in soft finesse.

Beneath the boughs, a world apart,
Whispers echo in the heart.
Branches cradle, leaves enfold,
Tales of life in green are told.

In the canopy's expanse,
Dappled light begins its dance.
A leafy hug, a calm retreat,
The forest floor beneath our feet.

Wildheart Meditation

In the quiet woods, hearts beat,
Rhythms wild, yet calm and sweet.
Through the pines, a whispered prayer,
Nature's breath fills tranquil air.

Upon the moss, a soul at rest,
In the wild, we find our best.
Silent songs of streams we trace,
Here, we find our sacred place.

Pondering in nature's hold,
Stories of the wild unfold.
Deep in thought, a harmony,
Wildheart's call in symphony.

Breath of the Trees

Inhale deep, the forest's breath,
Life in green defies all death.
Through the leaves, a vital sigh,
Nature's essence, spirits fly.

Echoes dance on whispered air,
Every breath a bonding prayer.
Cradled in the wooded arms,
Find the stillness, shed alarms.

Each exhale, the trees align,
Nature's pulse becomes divine.
Breath of life in bark and leaf,
Timeless song, mankind's relief.

Sylvan Serenity

In twilight's gentle, silken glow,
Amidst the pines where soft winds blow,
Nature's whispers softly flow,
In sylvan serenity, hearts bestow...

Moonlight dances on the leaves,
As time's embrace forever weaves,
Dreams that twilight gently breathes,
In sylvan serenity, the soul believes...

Stars confide in night's embrace,
Silent as the thoughts they trace,
Mysteries of boundless space,
In sylvan serenity, we find our place...

Verdant Embrace

Through meadows kissed by morning dew,
A tapestry of emerald hue,
The world awakens, fresh and new,
In verdant embrace, spirits renew...

Beneath the canopy of green,
Where sunlight's threads weave soft and keen,
A gentle peace, serene, unseen,
In verdant embrace, hearts convene...

Rustling leaves in breezes play,
In light and shadows' soft ballet,
Nature's promise, come what may,
In verdant embrace, we find our way...

Whispering Leaves

Beneath the boughs where shadows dream,
In forest's hush, a sacred theme,
The secrets of the ages stream,
Through whispering leaves, a silent gleam...

Each rustle tells a tale of old,
Of whispered love in shades of gold,
A story in the twilight told,
Through whispering leaves, the heart's enfold...

In quiet shadows, softly stirred,
The echoes of the past are heard,
A song without a single word,
Through whispering leaves, the soul is spurred...

Emerald Reflections

By waters clear, where willows weep,
In silent watch, the forests keep,
A mirrored world in dreams so deep,
In emerald reflections, the secrets sleep...

The surface shimmers, gently still,
A canvas where the heart can spill,
Images that memory fills,
In emerald reflections, time stands still...

Glimpses caught in fleeting glance,
Of nature's tender, quiet dance,
A moment held in wistful trance,
In emerald reflections, dreams enhance...

Verdant Murmurs

In the hush of morning light,
Whispers of the forest speak,
Upon the leaves, secrets alight,
In emerald hues, souls seek.

Beneath the boughs, shadows play,
Dancing in a dappled trance,
Green silken whispers sway,
In nature's quiet dance.

Streams of light through foliage weave,
Glistening on dew-kissed leaves,
Ancient oaks their stories breathe,
In the verdant murmurs' eaves.

Softly singing, branches bow,
A serenade to the skies,
Each whispering leaf, a vow,
In the forest's gentle sighs.

Birds join in the woodland choir,
Chirping tunes of old and new,
Verdant murmurs never tire,
Echoes in the morning dew.

Quiet Canopy

Beneath the quiet canopy,
Leaves rustle tales untold,
Silent whispers, soft and free,
In the forest's heart of gold.

Sun-lit beams break through the green,
Lighting paths where wild things tread,
In the stillness, peace is seen,
By the canopy overhead.

Ancient trees with branches wide,
Shield the ground from burning sun,
A living tent, where dreams reside,
Until the day is done.

Below, the forest creatures roam,
In the shade of leafy veils,
Among the roots, they make their home,
As silence softly trails.

At dusk, the quiet deepens still,
Mystic shades in twilight's weave,
Underneath the branches' will,
Nature's secrets gently breathe.

Earth's Green Mantle

Wrapped in nature's verdant cloak,
Forests rise in endless green,
Where the heart of earth does spoke,
Life in every shade and sheen.

Beneath the mossy, emerald quilt,
Whispers of old stories creep,
Tales of lives entwined in silt,
In the forest's ancient keep.

Canopies of leafy arms,
Stretch to catch the morning light,
Safeguarding the earth's rich charms,
Ever watchful, day and night.

Through the boughs, a gentle hum,
Wind's soft breath through needles weaves,
Songs of nature ever come,
Rustling in the twilight eves.

Earth's green mantle shields and sways,
In a dance both wild and free,
Beneath its fold, all creatures blaze,
With the fire of life's decree.

Leaf-Laden Paths

Beside the leaf-laden paths,
Nature's beauty lies untamed,
Footsteps fall on autumn's bath,
In hues by sunlight framed.

Crisp and whispered underfoot,
Golden tales of seasons past,
Each step taken in pursuit,
Of memories that last.

Arches formed by boughs above,
Carve a shelter from the skies,
Within this haven, peace and love,
In the forest, softly lies.

Clustered leaves, a carpet laid,
On the trails where wanderers roam,
Every step, an homage paid,
To the earth that we call home.

Pathways wind through verdant aisles,
Guiding hearts on nature's quest,
Within these leaf-laden miles,
We find the solace of the blessed.

Into the Green Abyss

Deep within the emerald shade,
Mysteries in silence laid.
Footfalls soft on mossy ground,
Whispers of the lost resound.

Vines entwine in ancient dance,
Shadows weave a fleeting trance.
Beneath the canopy, dreams revive,
In the green, our souls arrive.

Hidden streams in secret flow,
Through the depths where echoes grow.
Each leaf holds a timeless lore,
Tales of those who've walked before.

Glimmers of light in darkest folds,
Nature's treasures, secrets told.
In the abyss, hearts renew,
Emerald depths, a verdant view.

Wander far and leave behind,
Worries of the world confined.
Into the green, find your bliss,
In the heart of the abyss.

Woodland Harmony

Between the trees, a song is sung,
Ancient words from ages long.
Birds and breezes blend the tune,
A symphony of afternoon.

Footsteps soft where shadows play,
Melodies in branches sway.
Nature's heartbeat, steady, pure,
In this realm, life's overture.

Streams entwine in rhythmic dance,
Leaves perform their gentle prance.
Every creature plays a part,
In this woodland's beating heart.

Harmony in hues of green,
Sounds that paint the unseen scene.
In this grove where echoes meet,
Find the cadence, pure and sweet.

Rest beneath the leafy boughs,
Feel the peace that nature vows.
In this place, all sorrows flee,
Woodland's song of harmony.

Forest's Caress

In the hush of ancient woods,
Where the mighty oak still stood.
Gentle sighs of wind's caress,
Nature's touch, a sweet finesse.

Velvet paths of earthen trails,
Ferns unfold in verdant tales.
Branches reach with tender grace,
Cradling life's embrace.

Sunlight filters, dappled light,
Golden beams in soft twilight.
Each caress a whispered song,
Nature's arms where we belong.

Wildflowers in colors grand,
Paints a picture, softly planned.
In the forest's warm embrace,
Every step a sacred space.

Lay your burdens, find your rest,
In the woodland's gentle breast.
Feel the forest's tender kiss,
Soft and warm, a sweet caress.

Leafy Whispers of Myth

Beneath the vault of canopy,
Lie whispers of eternity.
Legends in the rustling leaves,
Ancient tales the forest weaves.

Elves and sprites in shadows flit,
Magic in the moonlit grit.
Myths unfold in every breeze,
Secrets held by ancient trees.

Woodland fae in whispers speak,
Echoes from the mystic creek.
In the twilight, visions rise,
Tales as old as starlit skies.

Through the pines, a subtle call,
Magic woven over all.
Believe the lore of leaf and limb,
Myth and nature, lush and dim.

In this realm of leafy green,
Worlds unseen and tales between.
Step within and lose your breath,
In the whispers, find their myth.

Sighs of the Undergrowth

In shadows deep where secrets grow,
Silent whispers softly flow,
Through tangled roots that intertwine,
Nature's breath in hushed design.

Leaves like whispers gently fall,
Echoes of the forest's call,
Mossy realms where time stands still,
Soulful sighs the air does fill.

Glimmering beneath the shade,
Life's mysteries there portrayed,
Beneath the canopy so vast,
In the undergrowth, shadows cast.

Silent steps of creatures small,
In this realm where peace does sprawl,
Listening to the woodland's tale,
Sighs of life in every trail.

The earth below, a hidden trove,
With secrets only it can know,
In the quiet, life unfolds,
In the undergrowth's tender hold.

Melodies of Rustic Earth

Beneath the sky, so vast and wide,
Where horizon and dreams collide,
Rustic earth in tones of brown,
Melodies in silence drown.

Fields that stretch to touch the blue,
Whispers of winds that softly blew,
Songs of soil and grain and sun,
Life's rhythms in nature spun.

Gentle hums of evening light,
Crickets sing with stars in sight,
A chorus of the land profound,
Rustic tones in every sound.

Farmers' hands have tilled the land,
Songs of work and hearts unplanned,
In each note the earth does share,
Life and love beyond compare.

Echoes of the ancient loam,
Roots of life and seeds of home,
Melodies in silence stayed,
Rustic earth where dreams are laid.

Wildwood Serenades

In the heart of forest deep,
Where olden trees their secrets keep,
Wildwood serenades arise,
Songs that reach the moonlit skies.

Fairy wings and shadows play,
In the dusk of fading day,
Leaves that rustle tell a tale,
Of ancient times in every gale.

Owls' call beneath the night,
In the dark a soft delight,
Melodies of nature's choir,
In the wildwood, dreams aspire.

Streams that whisper, flowers hum,
Life in rhythms softly strum,
Symphonies no man has made,
Wildwood's timeless serenade.

Within the depth of green embrace,
Music found in every place,
The forest sings, both bold and shy,
A serenade beneath the sky.

Hidden Grove Whispers

In a grove where secrets lie,
Whispers float as breezes sigh,
Silent voices speak so clear,
To those who have the heart to hear.

Branches weave a story old,
In this haven, tales are told,
Of life and love and dreams past,
Hidden grove where shadows cast.

Flowers bloom with secret grace,
In their petals, time and space,
Softly murmuring to the wind,
Songs of worlds that once had been.

Cloaked in mystery, calm and still,
Whispers echo, hearts to fill,
In this grove where quiet dwells,
Nature's gentle story tells.

Step inside, let senses lead,
Hear the whispers, ancient creed,
In the grove, the world stands new,
With secrets whispered just for you.

Whispers of Evergreen

In the heart of the quiet glade,
Echoes of time softly played,
Leaves dance to the whispers low,
Nature's secrets softly flow.

Boughs of pine, with scent so sweet,
Underfoot, the mossy seat,
Silent woods with tales unseen,
Life thrives in each shade of green.

Sunbeams filter through the mist,
Softly touched by evening's kiss,
In this hush, a song is born,
Of nights and days forevermore.

Nestled deep in thoughts profound,
Nature speaks without a sound,
Echoed whispers, evergreen,
With a grace that's seldom seen.

Mossy carpets, gentle dreams,
Streamlets weave through woodland seams,
Each a verse in the earthly tome,
Whispers lead me gently home.

Shaded Solitude

In the grove where shadows play,
Light and dark weave night and day,
'Neath the leafy canopy,
Find a world of mystery.

Whispering winds through silent trees,
Nature hums in minor keys,
In the stillness, thoughts unwind,
Solitude for heart and mind.

Softly tread on earthen floor,
Ancient secrets to explore,
Dappled light and shade entwine,
Lost in moments, so divine.

Through the green and fleeting shade,
Spirit's call is lightly laid,
Hold me here in quiet peace,
Time suspended, troubles cease.

Shaded orb of nature's past,
Memories in shadows cast,
In this world of solitude,
Find a soulful interlude.

Realm of Quiescence

In a realm where silence reigns,
Peaceful groves and tranquil plains,
Gently sways the verdant field,
Secrets soft in silence yield.

Moonlit nights with stars aglow,
Quiet lakes where dreamers go,
In the hush of twilight's glide,
Find a calm where souls reside.

Whispers of a past serene,
Lie beneath the forest screen,
Echoes of a bygone time,
Softly sing in whispered rhyme.

Calm descends like morning dew,
Veiling all in silver hue,
Breath of life in stillness found,
Nature's heart in silence bound.

Realm of quiescence, pure and true,
Peace within the morning dew,
Here I find my spirit's rest,
Cradled in earth's gentle breast.

Green Velvet Paths

Winding through the ancient wood,
Paths of velvet where I stood,
Each step brings a story told,
Secrets hidden, ages old.

Cushioned trails of emerald light,
Guided by the soft twilight,
Wander here and delve so deep,
Into dreams the forests keep.

Sunbeams play on leafy bough,
Nature's murmurs; gentle vow,
Under skies so blue and vast,
Follow green velvet paths.

Feel the earth beneath your feet,
Heart and nature's chorus meet,
In the stillness, find your way,
Through the forest's soft array.

Green velvet paths of tranquil dreams,
Flowing like the quiet streams,
Leads us through the wild and tame,
Whispering each forest name.

Sylvan Echoes

In forests deep the whispers call,
A symphony of ancient thrall.
The leaves alight with stories told,
Of secrets vast and ages old.

Beneath the boughs where shadows play,
The breeze does dance, then slip away.
An echo of a time long past,
In sylvan glades, the memories last.

The brook flows on its ceaseless song,
Through mossy banks it winds along.
A gentle lull, a soft embrace,
In woodland depths, a sacred space.

Oh, listen close, the forest's plea,
A timeless cry for you and me.
To guard and keep its mystic lore,
And let its echoes ever soar.

So wander through this ancient grove,
With footsteps light, with heart to rove.
For in these woods, a soul can find,
A harmony of heart and mind.

Verdant Stillness

In fields of green, the silence dwells,
A quiet peace, where nature tells.
Of life renewed in every blade,
A tranquil realm in sunlight laid.

The leaves they whisper, soft and low,
Of emerald seas where calm winds blow.
No rush or haste disturbs their peace,
In verdant stillness, sorrows cease.

Each petal holds a world within,
A universe in green so thin.
Where life abounds in hushed delight,
And every dawn brings subtle light.

The grasses sway in rhythmic dance,
A gentle, soothing, wild expanse.
Their silent song a lullaby,
Beneath the vast and open sky.

So let us find this tranquil shore,
Where earth and heart can merge once more.
In verdant stillness, we shall find,
A respite for the weary mind.

Dappled Sunlight

Through leafy canopies it streams,
A light that dances, full of dreams.
With dappled touch on forest floor,
It weaves a tapestry of lore.

The sun's embrace in golden hue,
Paints life anew in every view.
In shadows cast and light's display,
It whispers secrets of the day.

A play of light, a tender kiss,
In moments pure, of tranquil bliss.
Where sunbeams break through verdant green,
To grace the world with gentle sheen.

Each ray a thread in nature's weave,
Where earth and sky in union cleave.
A symphony of light and shade,
In dappled sunlight, life is made.

So walk this path where wonders lie,
Beneath the boughs, under the sky.
And feel the magic softly bright,
Of nature's art in dappled light.

Green Refuge

In glades where light and shadow meet,
There lies a refuge calm and sweet.
A sanctuary from life's haste,
In green embrace, no moment's waste.

Where ferns unfurl in sheltered nooks,
And silence dwells in babbling brooks.
The world outside seems far away,
In green refuge, the heart can sway.

Each leaf a balm, each breath a song,
In this embrace, where we belong.
The hustle fades, the worries die,
As peace descends from leaf and sky.

Here in this grove where stillness grows,
A solace deep, the spirit knows.
In green embrace, a whispered prayer,
That we might always find it there.

So seek this refuge in the wild,
With open heart and spirit mild.
For in its arms, we come to find,
A healing touch for heart and mind.

Green Symphony

In fields where wildflowers grace the breeze,
Lush symphonies of emerald trees,
Nature's orchestra takes its stand,
In the bounteous, verdant land.

Chirping crickets join the tune,
Beneath the silver, glowing moon,
A chorus of the night is born,
Till the blush of early morn.

Rivers whisper ancient tales,
Rolling through the misty vales,
Their currents dance in endless rhyme,
Echoing through space and time.

Leaves rustle in a soft caress,
Nature's touch, a sweet finesse,
Every branch and blossom sways,
Cloaked in green of summer days.

Birdsongs melt into the air,
Melodies beyond compare,
In the symphony of green,
Life in harmony is seen.

Nature's Ballroom

Beneath the canopy's embrace,
Beams of sunlight interlace,
Trees align in grand display,
Welcoming the break of day.

Flowers bloom in radiant hue,
Petals soaked in morning dew,
In this ballroom wild and free,
Nature dances gracefully.

Bees in gold with treasured zest,
Sip from blossoms' vibrant crest,
Their buzz a tune that fills the hall,
Inviting creatures one and all.

Butterflies in colors bright,
Weave through spaces, gift of flight,
Painting arcs in silent cheer,
As they waltz through crystal air.

Leaves swirl down in dappled rain,
Joining in the sweet refrain,
In this ballroom of the wild,
Nature's wonders, soft and mild.

Whispering Woods

In the heart of whispering woods,
Secrets shared in ancient hoods,
Every tree and fern aligned,
With the whispers of the wind.

Paths of soft, forgotten earth,
Hold the traces of rebirth,
Twigs and leaves in shadows cast,
Tell the stories of the past.

Owls in daylight's quiet keep,
Guard the silence, pure and deep,
Their eyes are windows to the night,
Echoes of forgotten light.

Streams of sunlight filter through,
Painting scenes in golden hue,
Where the forest breathes and weaves,
Tales of autumn's fallen leaves.

All around, a mystic hum,
Nature's voice in softest drum,
In the woods where whispers blend,
Every breath, a timeless friend.

Roots and Rivers

Roots dig deep in earthen beds,
Binding soils where life is fed,
Drinking from the streams that pass,
Carving paths through dewy grass.

Branches stretch towards the skies,
Reaching out with silent sighs,
With each season's ebb and flow,
Where the rogue rivers go.

Waters glisten in the light,
Racing on with pure delight,
From the mountains to the sea,
In their own wild jubilee.

Roots and rivers, time's embrace,
Ever running in the race,
Nature's pulse in rhythm speaks,
In the valleys and the peaks.

Here the essence intertwines,
Roots below and rivers' lines,
In the dance of life they find,
Eternal ties that nature binds.

Tranquil Thicket

Leaves whisper secrets, calm and pure,
Beneath the canopy's embrace.
Morning dew, a silent lure,
Nature's quiet, sacred place.

Sunlight dances, golden beams,
Painting shadows, soft and slow.
In this realm of ancient dreams,
Time itself forgets to flow.

Birdsong weaves a melody,
Gentle, sweet, and clear.
Within the thicket, harmony,
A sanctuary from all fear.

Moss on stones, a velvet green,
Pillows for the wandering heart.
Mysteries in silence seen,
In this woodland, set apart.

Paths meander, lost in thought,
Eclipsed by nature's gentle sigh.
In the thicket, peace is sought,
Beneath the endless, open sky.

Green Haven

Beneath the arch of verdant leaves,
Lies a world untouched by man.
Where every spirit softly weaves,
Their stories in a timeless span.

Rivers murmur ancient songs,
Flowing free and wild.
In this haven, nothing wrongs,
Innocence, undenied.

Canopies of emerald hue,
Shade the forest floor.
Each whisper of the breezy blue,
Invites you to explore.

Flowers bloom in silent grace,
Scatter scents so sweet.
Green Haven is a sacred place,
Where hearts and nature meet.

Thus, with every step, you find,
A solace so profound.
In Green Haven, leave behind
All worries, without a sound.

Serene Woodscape

The forest breathes a gentle sigh,
Whispers of a tranquil day.
Beneath the ever-changing sky,
Moments softly drift away.

Sheltered by the ancient trees,
Time stands still in quiet grace.
Here amidst the woodland breeze,
Find a calm, secluded space.

Shadows play on leaves entwined,
Patterns dance across the ground.
In this woodscape, peace you'll find,
Where the silence is unbound.

Birds compose their melodies,
Echoes of a life serene.
Every note and every breeze,
Paints a world of evergreen.

Walk the paths, let worries fade,
Harmony and light converge.
In this tranquil, leafy glade,
Feel the soul's renewal surge.

Murmuurs in Green

Soft murmurs through the forest glide,
Whispers in the emerald sea.
In every leaf, a secret hides,
Nature's tender symphony.

Flowing streams and rustling trees,
Compose a tune so pure and light.
In the green, the soul finds ease,
Guided by the heart's delight.

Glistening dewdrops on the fern,
Catch the morning's gentle gleam.
In the hush of dawn, discern,
Every silence tells a dream.

Footsteps echo on the trail,
Over moss so deeply lush.
In the green, where peace prevails,
Time and worries gently hush.

Murmuurs weave a seamless spell,
Binding hearts with nature's thread.
In the green, where wonders dwell,
Every murmur duly read.

Woods in Harmony

In the depths of forest green,
Where sunlight glimmers, soft and serene.
Birds chant high, a melody keen,
Nature's choir, a tranquil scene.

Leaves rustle in a gentle breeze,
Whispers of tales among the trees.
Roots entwined beneath, unseen keys,
Binding the earth in sacred decrees.

Streams weave through the woodland space,
Reflecting skies, a mirror's face.
Beneath the canopy's warm embrace,
The woods reveal their mystic grace.

Creatures wander, wild and free,
In this primeval tapestry.
Each step echoes a silent decree,
Of ancient woods in harmony.

Undergrowth Whisperings

Beneath the towering, aged oak,
Lies a world where secrets soak.
Whisperings in shadows cloak,
Stories awoken with a gentle stroke.

Mossy carpets, soft and thin,
Mysteries hidden deep within.
Silent murmurs, they begin,
In the undergrowth, where shadows spin.

Roots like veins in the forest's bone,
Carrying whispers, never alone.
Nature speaks in a tender tone,
In whispers of the undergrowth zone.

Life thrives in shadows and shade,
In the symphony that the wild has made.
Each whisper, a timeless serenade,
In undergrowth where stories pervade.

Songs of the Treeline

At the edge where sky and forest meet,
Nature hums a cadence sweet.
Songs of the treeline, a rhythmic beat,
Echoes that time cannot defeat.

Branches sway in a dance with the wind,
A ballet that the heavens rescind.
Leaves whisper secrets they've pinned,
Ancient truths they softly rescind.

Birds soar with notes so clear,
In harmony that all can hear.
Their symphony, devoid of fear,
Fills the treeline with chords so dear.

Twilight casts a golden glow,
As shadows stretch and breezes flow.
Songs of the treeline, soft and slow,
A lullaby where wonders grow.

Foliage Fantasies

Colors burst in a vibrant spree,
In the woodland's verdant sea.
Foliage fantasies, wild and free,
A palette of nature's grand decree.

Golden hues of autumn's kiss,
Emerald whispers in summer's bliss.
In spring, a flowery abyss,
Winter's bare branches add to this.

Sunlight dances upon each leaf,
Crafting images, bold and brief.
In this land, free of grief,
Foliage dreams offer relief.

Paths wind through this canvas grand,
Nature's art at every hand.
In foliage, where wonders stand,
Imagination finds its land.

Whispered Tales of Wood

Among the ancient, towering trees,
Where whispers hum along the breeze,
Old stories told in bark-rust tones,
Through leaves that flutter, sigh, and moan.

Deep roots entwined in earthen bed,
A symphony of greens and red,
Echoes of times now long forgot,
In shadows where the ferns have sought.

Moonlight spills on mossy ground,
Glimmers where the tales are found,
Branches twist in silent dance,
In the forest's timeless trance.

Listen close, the wood has more,
Secrets of its woodland lore,
Songs of streams and rivers wide,
Nature's hymn is forest's pride.

The heart of wood, a keeper keen,
Of memories in verdant sheen,
Each rustle, a testament,
To stories through the ages sent.

Verdure Beyond Horizons

Gaze upon the emerald sea,
Rolling hills of lush decree,
Boundless fields that stretch afar,
Underneath the sky's grand bazaar.

Sunlight dances on the leaves,
Whispers of the summer breeze,
Verdant waves in endless flow,
Where the meadow's blossoms glow.

A horizon draped in verdant hues,
Breathing life in morning's dews,
Boundless green in soft caress,
Nature's open, vast address.

Mountains rise in green embrace,
Forests thrive in sacred grace,
Breath of life in every blade,
In this realm where dreams are made.

Follow paths of whispered green,
To places where the soul is seen,
In the hug of flourishing lands,
Nature cradles in her hands.

Under the Leafy Eaves

Beneath the leafy, dappled shade,
In hidden nooks where dreams are made,
A canopy of emerald hue,
Shelters whispers, fresh and new.

Branches weave a living lace,
In this quiet, sacred place,
Birdsong mingles with the breeze,
In the realm beneath the trees.

Soft lights filter, golden, meek,
Through the cracks of foliage sleek,
Nature's chorus, soft and low,
In the peaceful, verdant glow.

Footsteps light on mossy floor,
Among the ferns and forest lore,
In each step, a tale unfolds,
In the greenery that enfolds.

Rest here, find the calm and peace,
Where the worries slowly cease,
Under leafy, tranquil eaves,
Where the heart in nature cleaves.

Primordial Green Respites

In the heart of primal green,
Time and life converge, serene,
Ancient breaths of verdant spires,
Whisper secrets, old desires.

Silence wraps in sage's shroud,
Underneath the leafy cloud,
Ferns and moss in history steeped,
In their verdant stories seeped.

Timeless trees in quiet pride,
Guard the tales of time's long tide,
In every bark and broken bough,
The echoes of the past endow.

Wanderers in green embrace,
Find the peace of nature's grace,
In primitive and wild domain,
Where ancient spirits still remain.

Here amidst the timeless green,
One can find the soul's serene,
In the shade of age-old heights,
In these primordial respites.

Woodland Zen

Beneath the canopy of ancient trees,
Whispers of winds, a gentle breeze.
In shadows dappled, light plays keen,
Nature's temple, serene unseen.

Moss carpets soft, underfoot delight,
A symphony of green, in morning light.
Birds' melodies, a sweet refrain,
Harmony found in woods again.

Leaves rustle softly, secrets they share,
A world unspoiled, without a care.
Streams weave stories, in stone's embrace,
Tranquil moments, in nature's grace.

Twilight descends, colors fade away,
Peaceful whispers as night meets day.
Stars above, through branches seen,
Woodland's lullaby, calm and serene.

Steps grow silent on this sacred ground,
In forest's heart, pure zen is found.
Breathing in the woodland air,
Find yourself, transcendent, there.

Hushed Earth Symphony

In twilight's glow, earth's melody rings,
Softly echoing, in whisperings.
Crickets sing, a nocturnal tune,
Under the gaze of a silver moon.

Tides of twilight, gentle and slow,
Breathe in the night like an ebb and flow.
Stars blink above, a celestial sea,
Part of the cosmic symphony.

Branches sway to the night's own song,
Nature's chorus, silent yet strong.
Hushed tones of night, in shadows deep,
Lull weary hearts into peaceful sleep.

Night flowers bloom, with scents so sweet,
Silent notes in nature's feat.
Owl's call, a distant, soulful cry,
Completes the symphony of the sky.

Morning whispers on the horizon's edge,
A subtle promise, a dawn's pledge.
Yet the night's song remains in air,
A timeless echo, everywhere.

Evergreen Echoes

Pines sway gently in the mountain breeze,
Their whispers carried across the seas.
Echoes of yore in each needle green,
Tales of ages past, nature's screen.

Boughs hold stories in their silent grasp,
Of seasons turning, in time's clasp.
Winters cold and summers bright,
Evergreens stand, a constant sight.

Needles rustle with an ancient song,
Ever-present, tender, strong.
In their shadows, life finds peace,
A sanctuary where troubles cease.

Green giants towering, touching sky,
Witness to the days passing by.
Roots dig deep, hold earth tight,
A symbol of enduring might.

Through the seasons, come what may,
Evergreen echoes lead the way.
Timeless sentinels, forever green,
Nature's guardians, silent, serene.

Dreams of Cedar and Pine

In dreams of cedar and pine so tall,
Whispers of the forest do softly call.
Fragrances weave through the midnight air,
Stories of ancients, everywhere.

Hilltops crowned in green's embrace,
Eternal woods, a sacred space.
Cedar's breath, a mystical lore,
Soothing the soul to its core.

Shadows play beneath the trees,
Dancing with the evening breeze.
Soft murmurs of a stream nearby,
Gentle lullaby, sweet and sly.

Night falls, stars begin to gleam,
Casting light on each quiet dream.
Branches cradle a moonlit sky,
Guardians of the dreams that fly.

In these woods, where peace is found,
Nature's lull makes hearts astound.
Dreams of cedar and pine endure,
Tranquil, timeless, ever pure.

Nature's Hidden Oasis

In a grove where shadows play,
Whispers of the breeze convey,
Secrets of the earth's embrace,
Hidden in this sacred place.

Leaves and petals gently sway,
Sunlight's golden, fleeting ray,
Streams that weave in soft refrain,
Nature's voice in sweet sustain.

Birds sing bright in dawn's bloom,
Free from worry, free from gloom,
Life anew in morning's light,
Nature's wonder, pure delight.

Mossy stones and ancient trees,
Home to whispers, songs, and dreams,
Invitation to the soul,
To find peace and to be whole.

By this water, time stands still,
Calm reflections, gentle thrill,
Eden's echo in the mist,
Nature's hidden oasis, kissed.

Vetiver and Fern Musings

Vetiver's roots dig deep and true,
Holding secrets old, yet new,
Whispers through the leaf and frond,
Nature's spell, a timeless bond.

Ferns unfurl with tender grace,
Patterns ancient, soft embrace,
In the quiet, green and grand,
Memories weave through the land.

Subtle scents of earth and air,
Vetiver's touch, soft and rare,
Breathe the calm, escape the haste,
Heaven found in nature's taste.

Dew-kissed leaves on mornings fair,
Speak of dreams within their care,
Silent vows of hidden streams,
Crafting nature's woven dreams.

Vetiver and fern unite,
Green symphony in sunlight,
In their bond, a story flows,
Nature's tale, forever grows.

Soft Pine Needle Cushions

Step on paths of pine-refresh,
Needles lie in soft, sweet mesh,
Cushions made by nature's hand,
Gentle layers on the land.

Trees reach high to kiss the sky,
Guardians of the earth and nigh,
In their shadows, tranquil ease,
Softened steps through whispered leaves.

Sunlight filters through the boughs,
Marking time with golden vows,
Rest beneath their ancient frame,
Feel the peace and know no shame.

Fragrant needles, green and pure,
Blanket pathways, paths obscure,
Velvet carpets of the woods,
Cradling hearts and lifting moods.

Close your eyes and breathe in deep,
Nature's balm within you seep,
On soft pine needle cushions laid,
Find the solace gently played.

Journey Through the Thicket

Paths that wind and twist unseen,
Through the thicket lush and green,
Hidden worlds within the dense,
Nature's maze, a soft defense.

Brush and bramble, winding tight,
Filters shade and dapples light,
Secrets held in every nook,
Nature's tale, a living book.

Whispers, rustles, faint footfalls,
Life's small echoes in the thralls,
Creatures dart with eyes so keen,
Life's drama in the verdant green.

Venture deep, and you will find,
Peace and wonder intertwined,
In this tangle, raw and wild,
Journey's essence, nature's child.

Through the thicket, courage bold,
Wander paths of stories old,
In the labyrinth of trees,
Find yourself in nature's ease.

Woodland Stillness

Whispers through the ancient pines,
Echoes soft where silence reigns.
Steps on paths of tangled vines,
Nature's voice in hushed refrains.

Sunlight filters, golden beams,
Piercing through the leafy veil.
Fauna flits in twilight dreams,
Secrets spun in forest tale.

Breezes murmur lullabies,
Weaving through the emerald shade.
Silence broken by bird cries,
Patterns in the leaves displayed.

Mosses cradle fallen leaves,
Time suspended in their hold.
In this stillness, heart reprieves,
Finds a peace, serene and bold.

Woodland whispers, mysteries,
In the quiet, truths unfold.
Here the spirit wanders free,
In the stillness, we behold.

Nature's Sanctuary

Temples tall of towering trees,
Columns carved by nature's hand.
Choral songs float on the breeze,
Silent hymns of this green land.

Waters crystal, mirrors made,
Reflect the skies' cerulean hue.
Life in shades of every glade,
Each leaf whispers something true.

Flowers bloom in vibrant hues,
Petals soft as summer dawn.
Gentle rains renew, enthuse,
Canvas painted, warm and drawn.

Creatures small find shelter here,
In this haven, danger thaws.
Every shadow hides no fear,
Only calm within its laws.

Nature holds us, cradles close,
Heals the soul with unstirred air.
In this sacred, green repose,
Sanctuary, pure and fair.

Beneath Canopy Greens

Beneath the lush, protective green,
Life unfolds in twilight's keep.
Shadows dance, a soft unseen,
Where the woodland secrets sleep.

Dappled light through branches weave,
Etching stories with their glow.
Whispered words, we must believe,
In this realm where wonders grow.

Footsteps soft on mossy bed,
Echo not, disturb them naught.
Silence here by shadows led,
Every peace by stillness taught.

Leaves converse in whispered tones,
Tales of times and seasons past.
Rooted deep, their ancient bones,
Hold the memories to the last.

Through the canopy, we stray,
Find a world where peace is seen.
In this quiet, gentle sway,
We are one with canopy green.

Verdant Retreat

Step into the verdant bower,
Escape the toils of daily grind.
Here each leaf and every flower,
Whisper peace to troubled mind.

Paths of emerald softly wind,
Through this world of vivid dreams.
Where the heart its pulse may find,
Calm beneath the sunlight's beams.

Trickling streams in silver flow,
Breathe a song both pure and free.
In their currents secrets show,
Nature's symphony we see.

Lush and green, this leafy throne,
Calls to those who seek repose.
In its depth, a world unknown,
Gentle winds and hidden prose.

Verdant is this vast retreat,
Canvas drawn in emerald hue.
Here the weary find their seat,
In this sanctuary, true.

Shaded Tranquility

Beneath the leafy canopy, stillness reigns,
A world untouched by time, free from pains.
Dappled sunlight dances on the forest floor,
Nature's quiet whispers, asking for more.

In this refuge, minds and hearts find peace,
An ancient lullaby that will never cease.
The rustling leaves sing songs of old,
Secrets in the breeze, stories untold.

Birdsong weaves a symphony, gentle and pure,
A tranquil aria that will forever endure.
Soft moss underfoot, a verdant dream,
Here, in shaded tranquility, souls redeem.

Streams wander lazily through the glade,
Glistening under a shifting, leafy shade.
A sanctuary where worries dissolve,
In nature's embrace, all problems resolve.

As twilight whispers its gentle goodnight,
The forest hums with a peaceful light.
Beneath the stars, the quiet persists,
In shaded tranquility, true joy exists.

Timber Temples

Columns of cedar rise, ancient and grand,
Guardians of secrets in this timeless land.
Silent sentinels with roots deep and wide,
In timber temples, serenity abides.

A cathedral of green, where sunlight streams,
Through stained glass leaves, casting golden beams.
Whispers of wind, a hymn soft and sweet,
In the heart of the forest, where souls meet.

Under their branches, a cool, calm embrace,
An eternal shelter, a sacred space.
Nature's sanctuary, untouched and pure,
In timber temples, peace is sure.

Roots intertwine like veins of the earth,
A testament to resilience, rebirth.
In the stillness, wisdom quietly speaks,
Answers in the silence that everyone seeks.

As twilight descends, a gentle twilight call,
Shadows stretch long, as night begins to fall.
In these hallowed halls, life slows to rest,
In timber temples, hearts find their best.

Sunbeams and Shadows

Sunbeams twinkle through the canopy's veil,
Creating a dance, a light-touched trail.
Shadows respond with a somber grace,
Nature's theater, an enchanting place.

In this play of light, stories unfold,
Tales of warmth and mysteries untold.
Each shifting shade, a fleeting embrace,
In sunbeams and shadows, a gentle chase.

Leaves flutter softly in the golden light,
Casting fleeting moments, a delicate sight.
A symphony of contrasts, day's gentle ebb,
Nature weaving magic with a silken web.

The forest becomes a mosaic of hues,
Blending the day's lively, muted cues.
Each shadow a pause, each sunbeam a clue,
In this serene interplay, the old and the new.

As the sun dips low, painting the sky,
Shadows lengthen, bidding day goodbye.
In the mix of twilight's final glow,
Sunbeams and shadows, a delicate show.

Lush Awakening

Morning dew kisses the leaves anew,
A verdant world awakening to view.
Birdsong heralds the break of dawn,
In lush awakening, a day is born.

Flowers unfurl in a vibrant display,
Greeting the sun, welcoming the day.
Each petal a promise of life's rebirth,
A tapestry of beauty, a gift to the earth.

The forest stirs with a gentle sigh,
As nocturnal creatures bid night goodbye.
A symphony of life begins its play,
In this lush awakening, all come to stay.

Sunbeams filter through the emerald green,
Creating a world so serene, unseen.
In every corner, life starts to bloom,
Dispelling the night's lingering gloom.

As the day unfolds in a radiant sweep,
Nature's pulse quickens from its deep sleep.
In the heart of the forest, joy is remade,
In lush awakening, dreams never fade.

Unseen Woodland Elegies

In shadows deep where secrets dwell,
A whisper on the breeze's tongue.
The forest keeps its timeless spell,
Where ancient songs are softly sung.

Beneath the canopy's embrace,
Old spirits dance in moonlit glades.
Their faces lost without a trace,
In twilight's soft and fading shades.

The leaves that fall like whispered sighs,
Are tales of those who walked before.
In unseen woodland elegies,
Their echoes stir forevermore.

Oft times the streams will gently weep,
For lives long past, for dreams once held.
In silent woods where secrets sleep,
Untold, in nature's realm compelled.

Heart of the Evergreens

In verdant seas where tall pines sway,
The heart of forest whispers clear.
Where light and shadow softly play,
And nurture dreams devoid of fear.

Within these woods, the world stands still,
A timeless dance of green and gold.
The wind's soft breath, the birdsong's trill,
A living story to unfold.

Each tree, a sentinel so wise,
With roots that delve and branches high.
They touch the earth, they scrape the skies,
Beneath their watch, the spirits lie.

Here in the heart of evergreens,
Life thrums in rhythm pure and bright.
With every hue, with every scene,
It paints the day, it shades the night.

Into the Silent Glade

Step lightly into silence deep,
Where sunlight sparsely filters through.
A hidden world where shadows creep,
In shades of brown and verdant hues.

The air is thick with hushed repose,
A stillness ancient, pure, and grand.
Where time in silent cycles flows,
Untouched by any mortal hand.

In corners where the mosses grow,
A carpet soft, a bed of green.
The forest's gentle secrets show,
In whispers felt but rarely seen.

Among the ferns, the flowers hide,
Their fragile faces turned away.
Into the silent glade we slide,
Where dreams and nature intertwine.

Beneath the Timbered Skies

Beneath the timbered skies we walk,
In canopies of leafy green.
Where ancient trees in silence talk,
And share their wisdom still unseen.

Their branches reach, their shadows cast,
A dappled dance upon the ground.
In forest's heart, the moments last,
And peace in nature's pulse is found.

Each step we take, a reverie,
In halls of wood, in realms of shade.
The whispering leaves, an elegy,
In arbored skies, serenely laid.

Beneath these timbered skies we find,
A solace deep, a tranquil air.
In nature's arms our souls unwind,
In sacred woods, forever fair.

Leafy Whisperings

Beneath the ancient canopy, still and serene,
Leaves murmur secrets in a verdant sheen,
Dappled light dances in a ceaseless dream,
Nature's whispers in a green, gleaming theme.

The forest floor, a patchwork of moss and bark,
Holds stories of wanderers, fresh and stark,
A breeze carries tales, both old and new,
Leafy whisperings in hues of emerald hue.

Birdsong interlaces with rustling sound,
A symphony in green, where peace is found,
Each whisper a note in the tranquil air,
Nature's melody, beyond compare.

Sunlight filters through, a golden hue,
Casting shadows, creating forms anew,
Each movement a part of the whispered lore,
Leafy secrets, forevermore.

Into the grove, the green song weaves,
A quiet tale among the leaves,
Softly spoken between branch and bark,
In leafy whisperings, hearts embark.

Emerald Calm

In the stillness of the emerald shade,
Where sunlight and shadows gently trade,
A calmness dwells, serene and wide,
An emerald hush where dreams abide.

The branches sway in a rhythmic grace,
A tranquil dance in this quiet space,
Leaves flutter down like soft-spun lace,
In emerald calm, they find their place.

Silent waters reflect the trees,
Caught in the whisper of a breeze,
Nature's lullaby in endless reprise,
Emerald calm beneath the skies.

A hidden glen, where peace prevails,
Among the trees and winding trails,
Silent and green, beyond the pales,
Emerald calm, it never fails.

In this haven of the woodland's heart,
Where tranquility plays its subtle part,
Time slows down, life's worries depart,
In emerald calm, we find our start.

The Green Mosaic

A tapestry woven by nature's hand,
In shades of green across the land,
Each leaf, each blade, a piece to play,
Together they form the green mosaic's way.

Among the trees, a patchwork spread,
Where every bough and branch is wed,
To the earth below, roots deeply fed,
The green mosaic, where life is led.

Ferns and vines in intricate dance,
Create a scene that holds our glance,
A living quilt of circumstance,
The green mosaic's vast expanse.

Every color of the forest floor,
A tile in the endless lore,
Of life that thrives and soars,
In the green mosaic, evermore.

Above, the sky a distant blue,
Beneath, the green in every hue,
A world united, old yet new,
The green mosaic, through and through.

Elven Quietude

Amidst the forest, where shadows play,
In realms where whispers gently sway,
An elven calm, serene, holds sway,
Quietude in the light of day.

The rustle of leaves, a gentle song,
Echoes where the heart belongs,
In elven woods, both deep and long,
Quietude where silence is strong.

Moonlight bathes the ancient trees,
In silver glow, a timeless freeze,
Elves tread softly, with utmost ease,
Quietude beneath the breeze.

By the brook, where waters flow,
Elven songs in murmurs go,
A tranquil hymn, both high and low,
In quietude, the spirits show.

This enchanted peace, a rare delight,
In shadows cloaked, both day and night,
Elven quietude, soft yet bright,
A sanctuary of gentle might.

Timber-Whispered Tales

In forests deep, where shadows dance,
Whispers glide in moonlit trance,
Leaves tell stories, old and frail,
Silent truths on every trail.

Echoes weave through ancient bark,
Veins of time, through light and dark,
Timber creaks a gentle song,
Nature's secrets, pure and strong.

Moss-clad roots in twilight glow,
Hold the tales of long ago,
Soft the breeze, with stories filled,
Woodland legends, heart instilled.

Boughs bend low to pass the word,
Heartfelt murmurs quietly heard,
Songs of old in windswept calls,
Forest whispers, through the halls.

Journey through this verdant lore,
Find the tales from days of yore,
In each leaf and shadowed vale,
Live the timber-whispered tale.

Glimmering Green Shadows

Emerald hues in sunlight's sheen,
Glimmering shadows seldom seen,
Dappled light through canopy,
Glows with nature's tapestry.

Golden flecks on verdant floor,
Whispered secrets evermore,
Blending hues of green and gold,
Stalwart guardian strong and bold.

Beams descend through leafy veil,
Casting shapes in twilight pale,
Silent whispers, softly told,
Treasured moments here unfold.

Mossy branches, shadows dance,
Nature's hush, a silent trance,
In the stillness, magic gleams,
Life reflects in shaded dreams.

Wander deep where shadows play,
Hear the songs the leaves convey,
In the glimmering green below,
Nature's secrets freely flow.

Branching Solitude

Silent paths of earthen grace,
Branching out in open space,
Lonely trees in forest deep,
Secrets in their stillness keep.

Echoes in the quiet wood,
Language only silence could,
Translate from the rustling leaves,
Timeless tales the wind retrieves.

Every limb, a solemn prayer,
Reaching skyward, open air,
Rooted in the tranquil earth,
Yet in solitude, their worth.

Shade and sunlight interlace,
Offering a quiet place,
For the heart to find its peace,
In the stillness, whispers cease.

Solitary, yet they stand,
Silent guardians of the land,
In their calm and quietude,
Find the peace of branching solitude.

Emerald Solstice

In the height of summer's blaze,
Emerald suns in leafy maze,
Halcyon days in green array,
Solstice brings the longest stay.

Verdant crowns in sunlight gleam,
Whispered songs upon the stream,
Nature's choir in warm embrace,
Harmony in shaded place.

Light and shadow softly blend,
Seasons whisper, summer's friend,
Extended days in verdant glow,
Timeless dance in ebb and flow.

Emerald hues in summer's kiss,
Catch the sunlight's fleeting bliss,
From the dawn to twilight's shade,
Nature's solstice serenade.

As the earth in green resplend,
Steadfast roots and branches bend,
In the heart of summer's height,
Emerald solstice, pure delight.

Verdant Silence Rhythms

In the hush of morning light,
Where greenest leaves unite,
Nature's symphony plays soft,
In silence, spirits aloft.

Dew-kissed blades of grass,
Murmur secrets as we pass,
Each droplet holds a tale,
Whispered softly, without fail.

Sunlight dances on the stream,
Sparkling like a fleeting dream,
Birds join in sweet refrain,
Echoing joy, soothing pain.

Moss-clad boughs sway slow,
In rhythm with the forest's glow,
Heartbeats sync with the Earth,
In this realm of endless worth.

Veils of green embrace the soul,
In this peace, we find our goal,
Harmony in nature's arms,
Soothed by its tranquil charms.

Ravines of Respite

Hidden paths through shadowed glen,
Where light and dark weave again,
Steps echo in the hollow's core,
Find solace within nature's lore.

Streams carve whispers in the stone,
Ancient secrets, softly shown,
Wanderers find peace anew,
In these depths of verdant hue.

Leaves fall like silent prayer,
Touching softly, without care,
Nature's touch, a gentle guide,
In this refuge, hearts abide.

Caverns echo life once passed,
In their silence, hope is cast,
Rest beneath the rugged cliffs,
Feel the heart's gentle lifts.

Through the ravines, spirits soar,
Finding rest forevermore,
In the shadows, light is found,
In these depths, hearts are unbound.

Whispers Among Pines

Beneath the towering pine's embrace,
Where whispers find their secret space,
Wind carries tales of old,
In the forest, wisdom unfolds.

Needles brush the morning sky,
Songs of nature drifting high,
Each breath a story told,
In the wood's green and gold.

Sunrays filter through the leaves,
Golden threads that morning weaves,
In the shadows, dreams reside,
Amongst the pines, hearts confide.

Footsteps on the forest floor,
Echo stories evermore,
Silence bleeds through time and place,
Nature's rhythm, a soft grace.

Pine cones fall like dreams at dawn,
In their fall, new hope is drawn,
Whispers greet the morning light,
In the pines, all is right.

Cascades of Emerald Light

Waterfall of purest green,
In the forest, seldom seen,
Emerald light cascades down,
Nature's jewel, nature's crown.

Shimmering in the sun's embrace,
A dance of light in gentle grace,
Leaves of green and water's flight,
Merge in harmony's quiet might.

Rivers flow in liquid jade,
Under canopy, in the shade,
Waves reflect the verdant beams,
Dancing in the stream's own dreams.

Rock and leaf, a symphony,
Crafted in pure artistry,
Earth and water's sweet duet,
Nature's lovers never met.

In this cascade of emerald hue,
Find the heart's refresh anew,
Glimmering in forest's height,
In these falls, soul takes flight.

Earth's Quiet Corner

In a nook so softly hidden,
Where the flowers dream in bloom,
Nature's secrets gently bidden,
Whisper secrets from the gloom.

Softly sways the meadow grasses,
To the song of morning dew,
As the hours gently passes,
Life begins anew.

Sunlight filters through the canopy,
Painting leaves a golden hue,
In this space so calm, so canopy,
Heartfelt solace, just for you.

Birdsong threads the air with music,
Echoes of a world contained,
Moments fleeting, moments lucid,
In this quiet, life reclaimed.

Footfalls light on moss-clad pathways,
Lead to dreams and thoughts so bright,
In Earth's corner, still and always,
Peace resides in morning light.

Green Dreamscape

Verdant fields stretch wide, beneath a sky so blue,
Daisies dot the horizon, kissed by morning dew.
A tranquil sea of green, where the heart finds rest,
In this dreamscape serene, where life feels best.

Butterflies flutter by, on wings of gold and hue,
Dancing to the rhythm, of a world reborn and new.
Gentle hills roll onward, in soft undulating waves,
A canvas of nature, that the wind softly craves.

Sunbeams pierce the canopy, painting shadows bright,
An emerald sea of tranquility, basked in light.
Each leaf a story tells, of rain and sun and time,
In this green dreamscape vast, where life's pulse is prime.

Whispering willows sway, to the melody of earth,
In harmony profound, with joy and mirth.
As twilight kisses dawn, in colors bold and deep,
In this green dreamscape lush, where dreams softly seep.

Woodland Reverie

In the hush of whispered breezes,
Dreams wake softly from their sleep,
Where the forest gently pleases,
Souls that wander ever deep.

Leaves aflutter with the sighing,
Of the ancient oaken trees,
In their shades, time undying,
Moments drift with ease.

Streams that murmur secret stories,
Over stones both smooth and worn,
Nature's tales in myriad glories,
In the daylight's early morn.

Roots embrace the earth so tender,
Binding life to timeless core,
Here where spirits gently render,
Echoes of what's come before.

Lost in thoughts and woodland wonders,
Mind and heart align as one,
In this reverie that sunders,
All that weighs, 'til day is done.

Whispers of the Pines

Through the pine grove gently swaying,
Comes a whisper, soft and low,
Nature's song in silence laying,
Secrets meant for us to know.

Needles brush in green caresses,
Scent of resin fills the air,
With each breath the soul confesses,
Dreams and hopes that linger there.

Winds that weave their subtle patterns,
Wrap the heart in calming grasp,
In the pines where light it lanterns,
Nighttime stars in firm clasp.

Shadows dance with dappled brightness,
As the forest hums a tune,
In this place of sheer delightness,
Day turns gently into noon.

Pines that stand as silent sages,
Guardians of the forest's song,
In their whispers, timeless pages,
Speak of where we all belong.

Verdant Silence

In the green where silence tangles,
With the breath of morning light,
Nature's hush, it softly dangles,
Moments pure and ever bright.

Lush the leaves with dew adorning,
Glisten like the stars of night,
In this space of verdant mourning,
Heart and spirit reunite.

Paths of moss in softest padding,
Lead to quiet pools of grace,
Where the world with no erratic cladding,
Finds its still and gentle place.

Echoes in the shadows drifting,
Songs of earth in whispers sweet,
In the silence ever sifting,
Hopes and dreams where heartbeats meet.

Gentle breezes stir the calmness,
Of the forest's emerald sea,
Here within this verdant paleness,
We find home, and we are free.

Dappled Light Hues

Underneath the filtered gold,
Shadows dance in patterns old.
Leaves in whispers gently speak,
Of secrets hidden, hours sleek.

Morning breaks with silvered rays,
Light and leaf in tender plays.
Emerald robes sway in breath,
To life's soft, unspoken depth.

The forest floor in mosaic spread,
A quilt of green and earthy tread.
Sunlight peeks through canopies,
In a mosaic of twilight seas.

Whispers of the twilight breeze,
Bring the dance of nature's ease.
Eyes embrace the serene sight,
Of dappled hues in soft daylight.

Evening sings in muted tones,
As twilight dons the twilight throne.
Shadows stretch and softly fuse,
In a painting of dappled hues.

Symphony of Sap and Bark

In the hush of early morn,
Ancient trees stand and adorn.
Each with stories deeply traced,
In the bark that's moonlit graced.

Whispers of the sap within,
Carry tales of where they've been.
Roots entwined in earth's embrace,
In this timeless, sacred space.

Leaves rustle in a melody,
Of the forest's living psaltery.
Nurtured by the soil's embrace,
A symphony in nature's grace.

Branches stretch in morning's glow,
Hooked to memories long ago.
Whispers of the winds so stark,
Echo the symphony of bark.

Harmony of nature's lay,
In the light of breaking day.
Sap as blood, and bark as skin,
Songs of life in whispered din.

Silent as the evening falls,
The forest breathes, and softly calls.
Songs of sap and bark compiled,
In nature's symphony, beguiled.

Quiet Arboreal Moments

A quiet hush in forest's core,
Whispers secrets evermore.
Morning dew on leaf and twig,
Shimmer, dance in nature's jig.

Underneath the verdant shade,
Peace and stillness gently laid.
Birdsong mingles with the breeze,
In these arboreal symphonies.

Sunlight sifts through hearty bough,
Lighting ferns in silken glow.
Crickets hum their hidden psalm,
In this wood, so cool and calm.

Fleeting shadows cast by wings,
As silence learns what morning brings.
Moments weave in tranquil thread,
Where earth and sky in whispers wed.

Evening's mist begins to curl,
In the branches' sheltered swirl.
Quiet moments held so dear,
In nature's heart, they're ever clear.

In the Lap of Tall Oaks

Majesty of wooded spire,
Tall oaks reaching ever higher.
Crowned with leaves in verdant gold,
Secrets of the ages told.

Roots entwined in earth's caress,
Grasping time in their finesse.
Winds they've faced and storms embraced,
In bark and leaf, they're interlaced.

Underneath their lofty shade,
Dreams of centuries gently laid.
Whispers trace each rugged line,
Of oak and sky in tranquil bind.

Mighty branches strong and wide,
Hold the sky, the stars inside.
In their lap, the world finds rest,
Cradled close to nature's breast.

Even as the twilight clings,
Oaks stand firm, like ancient kings.
In their shadow life reposes,
Where the heart of earth encloses.

Nature's Lullaby

Underneath the twilight, where the soft winds roam,
Nature sings a lullaby, calling all hearts home.
Crickets play a serenade, in the twilight dim,
A chorus of the forest, in a tranquil hymn.

Rustling leaves tell stories, of seasons come and gone,
With a gentle cadence, till the break of dawn.
Moonlight casts a tender glow, kissing night's retreat,
In nature's lullaby, where peace and dreams meet.

Flowing streams whisper secrets, to the silent night,
Reflecting the stars, in a dance of light.
Birds hush their chatter, as the night grows deep,
Cradled by the earth, all creatures drift to sleep.

Softly hums the meadow, a melody so pure,
In the cradle of the night, dreams find a cure.
Nature's lullaby, an embrace so wide,
In its gentle serenade, love and peace reside.

Enchanted Grove

In the heart of the forest, where mysteries unfold,
Lies an enchanted grove, with wonders untold.
Trees whisper secrets, in the rustling light,
In the grove's embrace, where day meets night.

Flowers bloom in magic, with hues so rare,
Perfuming the air, with a fragrance fair.
Faeries dance in twilight, under the moon's soft gleam,
In the enchanted grove, where dreams interweave.

Ancient trees stand tall, guardians of the past,
Their stories etched in bark, in the shadows cast.
Streams of silver flow, under canopy's grace,
In this sacred haven, a timeless place.

Whispering winds sing, an ethereal song,
To the pulse of the earth, where spirits belong.
In the grove enchanted, reality fades away,
Leaping into dreams, where the heart can stay.

Camouflaged Tranquility

In the heart of the forest, where shadows play
Leaves whisper secrets to the end of day
Sunlight dapples the ground below
In the hush, a gentle breeze does flow

Trees wear hues, from green to gold
Nature's palette, a story told
In silence, the colors blend
Camouflaged tranquility, my mind to mend

Hidden paths, where mosses lay
A serene retreat, where spirits stay
Every twig, a tale unfolds
In this sanctuary, peace holds

Amidst the canopy's dance above
The harmony of life, a silent love
Every step, a gentle creed
In this forest, hearts feel freed

Whispers of water, a distant stream
Camouflaged tranquility, like a dream
Beneath the boughs, where shadows play
Find your soul, let worries sway

Undulating Shade Reflections

In twilight's grasp, where shadows sway
Reflections dance at the close of day
Ripples on water, a gentle wave
Undulating shades, a secret they pave

The mirror of night, with stars alight
Whispers of dusk take gentle flight
Moonlit caress on undulating tide
A symphony of shades, where dreams reside

Leaves in chorus, a rustling song
Each echo carries night along
Undulating shades, a murmured hymn
In darkness deep, where hopes begin

Echoes of dawn on morning's brink
Through shadows dark, new light does sink
Undulating shades of night and day
In the quiet, let your soul sway

Brushstrokes of twilight paint the sky
Reflections of night in a gentle cry
Bathe in the shade where peace is found
Undulating reflections, heart unbound

Whispers of the Wild

In the still of the night, a breeze softly calls,
Through the forest deep, where the ancient owl sprawls.
Whispers of the wild, tales woven in trees,
Nature's own reverie, carried by the breeze.

Moonlight dances on the leaves, casting a glow,
Shadows interlace, in a silent show.
Footsteps of creatures, echo far and near,
In this untamed symphony, where hearts find no fear.

Rivers hum a melody, flowing calm and sweet,
With each ripple's gentle touch, the earth's pulse beat.
Stars peek through the canopy, in sparkle and shimmer,
Guiding weary wanderers with their constant glimmer.

Ancient stones and moss, the guardians of time,
Echo fragments of whispers, in a long-lost rhyme.
Beneath the twilight's embrace, nature's secrets bloom,
In the whispers of the wild, within night's gentle gloom.

Evergreen Embrace

Beneath the pines, where needle beds spread
An evergreen embrace, in nature's stead
Companions tall, through the seasons' call
Silent sentinels, they watch us all

Emerald boughs, in winter's grace
Eternal green, a soft embrace
In summer's blush, and autumn's hue
Evergreen, the constant view

Soft whispers through branches high
A symphony beneath the sky
In the arms of forest green
Peaceful breathes, serene, unseen

The evergreens, with roots so deep
Cradle secrets for us to keep
Beneath their shade, a quiet repose
Nature's arms, where comfort grows

Through seasons four, they stand so true
In evergreen embrace, life renews
Find your solace, seek your space
Within the trees, an endless grace

Breath of the Spruce

In the northern woods, where spruces rise
The breath of life beneath azure skies
Their needles whisper tales untold
Of ancient times and nights so cold

Amidst the snow, they pierce the air
Green spires stand, so bold and fair
Breath of spruce in winter's chill
A vital life, where hearts stand still

Through seasons' change, they hold their might
Beneath their boughs, shadows alight
A fragrant breath of forest deep
In the stillness, where spruces keep

Soft whispers in the morning frost
Breath of the spruce, a world embossed
Nature's balm in verdant shade
Inhale deeply, let worries fade

In twilight's glow, they stand so grand
Spruce's breath on ancient land
Every breeze a tender kiss
From spruce to soul, in purest bliss

Sylvan Heartbeats

In the forest's hush, the heartbeats trace,
A rhythm pure, a tranquil grace.
Beneath the canopy, shadows weave,
A secret life in nature's sleeve.

Whispers of winds through ancient boughs,
Where silence wears its sacred vows.
Lush green tendrils, softly twined,
Pulse with life, amid the pines.

Sunlight dapples in golden streams,
Awakening the hidden dreams.
Roots that delve in earthen beds,
Cradle tales the woodland spreads.

Each leaf a fluttering sigh of peace,
In the sylvan heart, all worries cease.
Branches sway in serene embrace,
The forest hums with timeless grace.

Mysteries in mossy beds unfold,
With every breath, a story told.
Nature's symphony, pure and fleet,
In sylvan heartbeats, we retreat.

Whispering Leaves Symphony

In twilight's eve, the leaves they murmur,
A symphony growing ever firmer.
Gentle rustles, soft and clear,
Nature's melodies, to heart endear.

Each whisper rides on zephyrs light,
Caught in the kiss of fading light.
Harmony in dusk's embrace,
Leaves weave sounds, a calming grace.

Echoes of ancients in each tone,
Feel the magic, feel at home.
Rivers of air, through branches sweep,
Lulling all to peaceful sleep.

Through verdant arcs, the breezes glide,
Nature's secrets they confide.
Ephemeral notes, forever sway,
In leaves' whispers, night and day.

Life's fleeting tunes in foliage born,
Played until the break of morn.
In the symphony of whispering leaves,
Eternal solace the soul receives.

Harmonic Woodlands

Among the trees, a song does rise,
An ancient tune that never dies.
Birds and brook in concert play,
Harmonics in the light of day.

The breeze conducts through foliage grand,
A canopy orchestra, nature's hand.
Flutter and chirp in perfect time,
Woodland echoes, so sublime.

Roots and branches, deep and high,
Join the chorus to the sky.
The forest hums with life's own beat,
In harmonic woodlands, all complete.

Under moonlit silver beams,
Harmony flows like woven dreams.
Each creature adds its voice in tune,
Together sing beneath the moon.

In this realm where music's free,
Heart and nature in symphony.
Woodlands' song, forever near,
Harmonic magic, crystal clear.

Ephemeral Enchantments

In the glade where magic lies,
Moments flicker, fireflies.
Ephemeral as morning dew,
Enchantments whisper, soft and true.

Petals shimmer in moon's glow,
Casting spells where shadows go.
Transient beauty, fleeting still,
Hearts with wonder, they do fill.

Each breath of wind a fleeting kiss,
Tales of dreams, ephemeral bliss.
Nature's charms, elusive dance,
Glimmer in a wistful trance.

The night transforms with gentle hand,
Weaving through an ephemeral land.
Softly glow the skies above,
Filled with wonder, filled with love.

As dawn breaks, enchantments fade,
Memories in morning laid.
For a moment, magic bright,
Ephemeral, fades with light.

Elms of Echoing Peace

In twilight's gentle, whispered breeze,
Underneath the elms' vast eaves,
Softly hums a song of ease,
Where restless hearts find sweet reprieves.

Beneath the boughs, where shadows dream,
A river flows in silent streams,
Reflecting stars in twinkling beams,
Within this sylvan, tranquil theme.

Birdsongs drift in mellow rays,
Through leafy canopies they play,
Their melodies in twilight's haze,
Dispel the night, welcoming day.

Here in this serene domain,
Whispers echo, free from pain,
Nature's harmony, softly lain,
In the elms of peace we gain.

Silent night descends so clear,
Cradling dreams without a fear,
In these elms of peace, hold dear,
Every whisper, close and near.

Emerald Passage

Through forest paths where shadows play,
In emerald hues of dawning day.
The canopy a living dream,
Where sunlight's golden fingers gleam.

Mossy stones and ancient trees,
Whisper tales upon the breeze.
A river's voice, a soothing sound,
In nature's heart, pure peace is found.

The ivy climbs in silent grace,
Embracing earth's eternal face.
Emerald passage, green and deep,
Where secrets of the forest sleep.

Sunset Through Cedars

Amber skies paint the horizon wide,
As daylight waves its sweet goodbye,
Through cedar branches, shadows glide,
In hues where golden moments lie.

The forest whispers evening's song,
As birds of dusk do sing along,
Through cedar scent, where dreams belong,
Fading light but never wrong.

Each leaf a canvas in twilight's hand,
Bathe in colors rich and grand,
Where night meets day on twilight's land,
Among the cedars where we stand.

As stars begin their radiant show,
Night's soft embrace begins to grow,
Through cedars, whispers gently flow,
In this serene, enchanted glow.

Beneath this sky of merging light,
In cedar's shade, embrace the night,
Till dawn returns with promise bright,
In the sunset's gentle flight.

Lichen-Laden Reveries

On mossy stones where silence grows,
Lichen forms in soft repose,
A tapestry of dreams bestows,
In nature's hidden, quiet shows.

Whispers of time on barkless trees,
Lingering in the summer breeze,
Tell tales of ancient mysteries,
In lichen-laden reveries.

Veils of green on forest floor,
Soft as clouds and nothing more,
Of slumbering realms they do implore,
In tranquil dreams forevermore.

In shaded glades where sunbeams weave,
Twilight whispers as we grieve,
Yet find solace, to believe,
In lichen's ancient, silent reprieve.

Through seasons' changing, endlessly,
These emerald tendrils, wild and free,
Speak in tongues of old, to me,
In lichen-laden reveries.

Caress of the Wildwood

Beneath the canopy, emerald light,
Whispers secrets of the night,
Where shadows dance in soft twilight,
In wildwood's tender, gentle might.

The breeze ensnares the fern's warm sigh,
As murmuring brooklets wander by,
In hint of mist, where dreams do lie,
Caressed by leaves, and boundless sky.

Each step you take on softened moss,
Is cradled in this world of gloss,
Where time stands still and cares are lost,
In wildwood's tender, verdant cross.

Through whispering pines and shaded groves,
The forest's soul in silence roves,
A realm where nature's grace behoves,
And every heart in love it hoves.

In wildwood's caress, find endless peace,
Where worries fade and burdens cease,
In this sanctuary, release,
Embrace the wild's serene increase.

Whispers Among Pines

In the stillness of twilight hours,
Pines stand vigilant and tall,
Their whispers, like ancient lore,
Tell secrets of the wood to all.

Soft breezes thread through needles thin,
Carrying stories far and wide,
Of creatures small and moments grand,
Where human eyes have never spied.

Each rustle is a quiet voice,
From nature's deep and hidden heart,
A language lost to bustling noise,
Yet in the silence, plays its part.

Under moon's gentle silver gleam,
The pines weave a lullaby,
A serenade to night's sweet dream,
Where shadows dance and spirits fly.

In the symphony of pines,
An echo of the world prevails,
Reminding us through earth's designs,
Of life in whispered, tender trails.

Emerald Canopy Dreams

Beneath the emerald canopy,
Where dappled sunlight filters through,
Dreams of nature come to be,
In hues of green and gold, they brew.

Leaves like emeralds sway and sigh,
Kissed by whispers of the breeze,
Painting visions in the sky,
With every rustle in the trees.

Dreamers find a haven here,
In the shade of forest's grace,
Where heartaches fade and skies clear,
And time's rush slows its pace.

Mornings bring a wakeful light,
To the dreams each leaf had spun,
Turning darkness into bright,
As the new day has begun.

In the canopy, life breathes,
With a rhythm old and true,
An eternal dance that weaves,
The dreams of green in every hue.

Sunlit Woodland Paths

Through sunlit woodland paths I tread,
Beneath the cloak of forest shade,
With each step, my worries shed,
As nature's splendor is displayed.

The sunlight dapples on the ground,
A golden mosaic in the leaves,
While the forest hums its mellow sound,
A symphony that softly weaves.

Trees like guardians line the trail,
Whispering secrets soft and low,
In their stories, truths unveil,
Of seasons past, of rain and snow.

Birdsong mingles with the breeze,
A chorus of the free and wild,
In this haven 'midst the trees,
We find the heart of nature's child.

Each path a journey to the soul,
A pilgrimage in quiet lands,
Where nature's touch makes whole,
As we walk, hand in hand.

Embrace of the Green Giants

In the embrace of green giants tall,
I find a peace that's seldom known,
Their shadows form a gentle wall,
A sanctuary overgrown.

Their branches stretch to skies so high,
A canopy that shelters dreams,
With every breath, a silent sigh,
Soft whispers lost in sunlit beams.

These giants hold the earth so tight,
Their roots entwined in deep embrace,
An ageless strength, a quiet might,
In the heart of this serene place.

Leaves that shimmer with the dew,
In the morning's tender light,
Recall the days of endless blue,
And stars that twinkle in the night.

Here, surrounded by their grace,
I'm cradled in a forest's arm,
In green giants' calm embrace,
Protected, safe from any harm.

Vernal Vibes

Spring whispers through the budding trees,
Where flowers dance on every breeze.
A chorus of the morning bright,
Enchants the day, ignites the night.

The brook, it sings a silver tune,
Beneath the watchful eyes of June.
Petals paint the earth anew,
In vibrant red, and softest blue.

Sunbeams waltz on meadows wide,
As nature's secrets swiftly glide.
Leaves unfurl with gentle sway,
In vernal vibes, we find our way.

Nature's Quiet Throne

Within the woods where silence reigns,
 A quiet throne that peace sustains.
 The whispers of the leaves unfold,
  In stories ancient and untold.

  Softly tread, the quiet ground,
 Where myriad lives in hush are found.
  Nature's quiet throne does stand,
   A palace of the serene land.

 The twilight brings a tender glow,
O'er hill and dale where wonders grow.
  Nature's sweep, a vast unknown,
    Infinite in its quiet throne.

In Green Solace

Beneath the lush, verdant embrace,
A world at peace, where troubles chase.
In green solace, time stands still,
A haven 'midst the rolling hill.

The scent of pine, the rustle light,
Day's slow fade to tranquil night.
Birdsong fills the forest air,
Serenity beyond compare.

Through dappled shade, the path winds on,
To realms where past and present dawn.
In green solace, hearts do mend,
In nature's arms, our spirits blend.

Tranquil Grove Wanderings

In the grove where whispers dwell,
Quiet murmurs cast a spell.
Leaves rustling, softly sway,
Guiding footsteps through the day.

Sunlight filters through the green,
A canopy of peaceful sheen.
Birds are singing overhead,
Nature's lullaby, gently spread.

Paths of moss and twigs entwine,
Leading hearts to lands divine.
Silence speaks in gentle tones,
Harmony in nature's bones.

Shadows play and light match wits,
Dappled calm where spirit fits.
Every step, a sacred grace,
In this tranquil, leafy place.

Softly now, the evening calls,
As moonlight through the treetops falls.
Stars adorn the velvet sky,
In the grove, my soul shall lie.

Verdant Sanctuary Moments

Within the verdant's warm embrace,
Find a haven, find the grace.
Grass beneath and sky above,
Wander here and feel the love.

Pine and cedar stand so tall,
Guardians of the woodland hall.
Flowers bloom with colors bright,
Painting days and pairing nights.

Gentle streams that whisper clear,
Echoing the stories dear.
Pebbles, smooth by nature's hand,
Tell of time across the land.

Ferns and ivy, winding free,
Create a world of majesty.
Breathing in the earthy scent,
In this sanctuary, hearts relent.

Moments here are timeless, pure,
In this land, find life's allure.
Serenity in every breath,
Nature's bosom till the death.

Moss-Covered Serenity

Mossy carpets, rich and green,
Cradle footfalls, pure and clean.
Speak of ages long since past,
In this realm where dreams are cast.

Shaded glens and glades serene,
Cradle whispers, unseen, keen.
Every corner, soft and whole,
Nurtures back the weary soul.

Ancient trunks and boughs so wide,
Embrace the world, side by side.
Quiet moments, hushed and still,
Bring the heart a gentle thrill.

Morning dew on velvet plains,
Catches light through window panes.
In the dance of sun and shade,
Peaceful memories are made.

Lay upon this mossy bed,
Rest your tired and weary head.
Find in quiet, greenest hearth,
Solace from the echoed path.

Echoes of the Ancient Trees

Underneath the ancient boughs,
Feel the timeless nature's vows.
Roots entwined in silent grace,
Stronghold of this sacred place.

Whispers from the leaves above,
Speak of life and lasting love.
Every breeze that stirs the air,
Carries tales, beyond compare.

Bark imprinted with the years,
Witness to both joy and tears.
In their shadow, calm descends,
History and present blend.

Echoes of the ages past,
Found in moments, still and fast.
Listen close, the stories ring,
From the heart of everything.

Underneath these ancient trees,
Find the soul's eternal keys.
Everlasting, deep, and free,
Live the echoes, wild and free.

Milton Keynes UK
Ingram Content Group UK Ltd.
UKHW022343200824
447185UK00013B/415